KNOW WHAT YOU'RE

F
O
R

A Strategy for Living the Life
God Wants You to Live

STUDY GUIDE | FIVE SESSIONS

JEFF HENDERSON

ZONDERVAN
REFLECTIVE

CONTENTS

I've spent a fair amount of my personal life and professional career trying to figure out what gets people's attention and what makes things grow. As a former marketing executive, I've worked with organizations like the Atlanta Braves and Chick-fil-A to help them figure out the best way to grow in their businesses. As a pastor at Gwinnett Church in Atlanta, Georgia, I've spent time figuring out how we as a church can contribute to the growth of our community and respond to individuals who come through our doors every week . . . while also challenging them to grow. As a parent and a husband, I'm definitely concerned about how to foster a home environment that encourages growth within the context of our ever-evolving family life.

Now, if you forced me to describe *growth* in a simple way that everyone could understand, I would point you to two key questions that we are going to discuss in this study. The first is: *What are you for?* The second question is: *What are you known for?* My experience is that these two questions are the catalysts for growth in businesses, organizations, churches, and in our everyday lives. So, during the course of this study, we are going to discover how those two questions can grow our work lives, our relationships, our community, and our world.

But more important, we are going to take a look at *who* and *what* God is for. All too often, people know more about what Christians are *against* rather than what they are for. My hope is this study helps you change that narrative for those in your world who think the church—and thus God—is against them. The Bible is clear we are to love others, extend grace, and get along as much as possible . . . and our actions speak louder than our words. "Just as you can identify a tree by its fruit, so you can identify people by their actions" (Matthew 7:20 NLT).

Here's the reason why I think this idea of being known for what you are FOR is so important: when you can articulate your answers to these two questions, it will not only grow your relationships, your business, your community, or your church, but it will also grow you and your influence as well. This is a revolutionary way to live and a powerful strategy for showing the world around you what you are for . . . and that you really are for them.

Jeff Henderson

The *Know What You're FOR* video study is designed to be experienced in a group setting such as a Bible study, Sunday school class, or any small group gathering. Each session begins with a welcome section, several questions to get you thinking about the topic, and a reading from the Bible. You will then watch a video with Jeff Henderson and engage in some small-group discussion. You will close each session with a time of personal reflection and prayer as a group.

Each person in the group should have a copy of this study guide. You may also want to have a copy of the *Know What You're FOR* book, as reading it alongside the curriculum will provide you with deeper insights and make the journey more meaningful (for your professional life and for you personally). The "For Next Week" section at the end of each between-sessions personal study lists the chapters in the book that correspond to material you are covering.

To get the most out of your group experience, keep the following points in mind. First, the real growth in this study will happen during your small-group time. This is where you will process the content of the teaching for the week, ask questions, and learn from others as you hear what God is doing in their lives. For this reason, it is important for you to be fully committed to the group and attend each session so you can build trust and rapport with the other members. If you choose to only go through the motions, or if you refrain from participating, there is a lesser chance you will find what you are looking for during this study.

Second, remember the goal of your small group is to serve as a place where people can share, learn about God, and build intimacy and friendship. For this reason, seek to make your group a safe place. This means being honest about your thoughts and feelings and listening carefully to everyone else's opinion. (Note that if you are a group leader, there are additional instructions and resources in the back of the book for leading a productive discussion group.)

Third, resist the temptation to fix a problem someone might be having or to correct his or her theology, as that's not the purpose of your small-group time. Also, keep everything your group shares confidential. This will foster a rewarding sense of community in your group and create a place where people can heal, be challenged, and grow spiritually.

Following your group time, reflect on the material you have covered by engaging in any or all of the between-sessions activities. For each session, you may wish to complete the personal study in one sitting or spread it out over a few days (for example, working on it a half-hour a day on different days that week). If you are unable to finish (or even start!) your between-sessions personal study, you should still attend the group study video session. You are still wanted and welcome at the group even if you don't have your "homework" done.

Keep in mind the videos, discussion questions, and activities are simply meant to kick-start your imagination so you are not only open to what God wants you to hear but also how to apply it to your life. So, as you go through this study, be watching for what God is saying to you as you discover a healthy strategy for living the life God wants you to live.

WHAT **F**
ARE **O**
YOU **R**

Everything you and I do as leaders is about people.
People want to know they matter.
People want to know we are FOR them.

JOHN MAXWELL

WELCOME

Today we are going to talk about two questions that I believe are essential for living the life God wants you to live: (1) *What do you want to be known for?* and (2) *What are you known for?* These questions are similar, but notice the subtle difference. The first is about what you *want* to be known for in your roles and responsibilities in life. The second is about what you are *actually* known for in your community. These two questions will not only affect your personal life but will also have the capacity to influence your relationships, community, and world—especially if you are willing to honestly assess the answers and make adjustments to close the gap.

I have the privilege of working with teams and leaders in businesses and community organizations. What I find is that these two questions have a huge impact in those spaces. Think of it this way. If a shoe company says they are for their customers, but they won't return a damaged shoe because of company policy, then who are they *really* for—the customers or the company? I'm guessing many of you have experienced this kind of "customer service."

On the flip side, I think about the story of an employee at a shoe company who spent six hours on the phone with a customer who had just lost her husband. When the call ended hours later, there was a budding friendship between the employee and the customer . . . but no shoe purchase. The leadership team at the company celebrated the employee anyway for *delivering happiness* (the company mission) to a customer in need. This is a great example of alignment between what the company *wants* to be known for and what they actually *are* known for.

Now, I realize that I am getting a little ahead of myself here. But I want you to hear this: *when you are known for one thing but talk about being known for something else, you lose credibility.* And once you lose credibility, you lose trust. Trust takes a lifetime to gain . . . but only a moment to lose. For this reason, we need to determine if these two areas are out of alignment. So, as we begin this study, let's have the courage to honestly ask these key questions and figure out how to close the gap. As we do, we will be committing to growth as individuals and as a community.

SHARE

If you or any of your group members are just getting to know one another, take a few minutes to introduce yourselves. Then, to kick things off for this session, discuss one of the following questions:

- What is your favorite role or responsibility in life right now?

 — *or* —

- What descriptive words do people use about you?

WATCH

Play the video segment for session one. As you watch, use the following outline to record any thoughts or concepts that stand out to you.

Notes
There are two key questions that can help grow your business, your organization, your career . . . and you as an individual.

> The first question is *what do you want to be known for?* What do you want to be known for in the roles and responsibilities of your life?

> The second question is *what are you known for?* This question is for the people in your life—what do they perceive to be your values, goals, and priorities?

Growth happens when the answers to these two questions match. You grow as a person but also in your roles and responsibilities in your business, your church, and your organization.

When the Son of Man comes, will he find faith on the earth?

JESUS (LUKE 18:8)

The reality is that none of us are perfect. There is going to be a gap between what you want to be known for and what you actually are known for. The goal is to close the gap!

These two questions can grow your business and your organization. What does your business *want* to be known for? What *is* your business known for? When the answers match, your customers experience your vision and tell others about your company.

The two questions can also grow your church. What does your church *want* to be known for? What *is* your church known for in the community? When the answers match, those who have said no to church in the past can realize the church is still saying yes to them.

In a hyper-cynical world that often is known for what it's *against*, let's be a group of people known for who and what we're *for*.

> Vision is like a bucket of water. The more words in the bucket, the more the vision spills out.
>
> JEFF HENDERSON

DISCUSS

Take a few minutes with your group members to discuss what you just watched and explore these concepts in Scripture.

1. Think about the first question: *What do you want to be known for?* This relates to the roles and responsibilities

that you have in your life. How would you answer this question?

2. Think about the second question: *What are you known for?* This relates to how other people in your world perceive your vision, goals, and priorities. How do you think they would answer this question?

3. In what specific area of your life might there be a gap between what you want to be known *for* and what you *are* known *for?* What areas of your life do you feel are in the greatest alignment between these two questions?

4. What factors do you think contribute to the gap or the alignment in your life? How would the people closest to you answer this question?

5. Read Acts 15:12–21. In this story, James, the brother of Jesus and leader of the church, was concerned about unnecessary barriers that were keeping people out of the church. How does this passage relate to what we are talking about today? What do you think are some of the barriers in the church today that turn people away?

6. What do you think the impact would be if people in the world really believed that the church was *for* them? What part could you play in making this happen?

RESPOND

Briefly review the outline for the video teaching and any notes you took. In the space below, write down the most significant point you took away from this session.

What specific action steps will you take this week to move toward what you want to be known *for*?

PRAY

Close your time together by praying for each other. Pray that God would clear up any confusion and help each one of you discover what you want to be known *for*. Ask God for the wisdom and self-awareness to pay attention to what you *are* known *for*. And if there's any disparity between the two, ask God to give you the courage to move toward more alignment in your life, as individuals and as a community. Write down any specific prayer requests in the space below so you can remember to continue praying throughout the week.

BETWEEN-SESSIONS
PERSONAL STUDY

Just as our cars need a regular tune-up and our bodies need physical therapy on occasion, our souls require realignment as well. In this session, we saw that most of us need realignment between what we're *for* and what we're *known for*. Start this process right this week by spending time with God each day and engaging in any of the following activities. Be sure to make any notes about the experience, as there will be time at the start of the next session to share any insights that you learned. In addition, if you have not done so already, you may want to read the prologue and introduction to the *Know What You're FOR* book.

FIND OUT WHAT YOU'RE FOR

Writer Annie Dillard says, "The way we spend our days is the way we spend our lives."[1] In other words, the small choices we make every day ultimately determine the way we live our entire lives. So, whether you are structured and methodical or spontaneous and full of variety in the way you spend your time, the things you do each and every day say something about who and what you're for. With this in mind, answer the following questions:

Consider your *personal and professional life.* What kinds of activities fill up your daily routine and your weekly or monthly rhythm?

What do you do when you have down time or a few free moments to yourself?

Take an honest assessment of your list. Is this how you want to be spending your time? If not, what things could you *stop* doing so you could *start* doing something else?

What does your list tell you about what you're *for*? Are you *for* the things you really want to be *for*? Explain.

Now consider the people around you. What do they say about the way you live your life? Is this what you want to be known for? Why or why not?

Where do you believe is the largest gap between what you say you're *for* and what others know you *for*? What are you going to do about that gap?

Read Romans 7:15–20. Paul understood this tension well—when you say you are for one thing but are known for something else. All of life on this side of heaven will be a constant push-and-pull to align your actions with your intentions. Sometimes you will manage the tension well, and other times you will struggle . . . as did Paul. Close your time in prayer by thanking God for the opportunities you've been given to discover what you're *for*. Ask him to give you the courage to act in a way so that what you're *for* is also what you're *known for*.

FOR OTHERS

Whether you spend your days in the boardroom, the classroom, or the living room, it's a pretty safe bet to say that everywhere you go people are watching how you live your life.

According to John Maxwell, the people you serve are constantly asking three questions about you and the way you show up with them:

1. Do you like me?
2. Can you help me?
3. Can I trust you?[2]

I've heard the staff at Gwinnett Church ask these questions of me, as well as the teams I've coached in business or out on the playing field. Even my own kids ask these questions of me. The truth is all kids want to know if their parents actually like them, if they can help them, and if they can be trusted. But here's the deal: remember, the first two questions aren't about *us* but about *them*. This is because people want to know they matter to us. People want to know we're *for* them. So consider how you make people feel when they're in your presence as you answer these questions:

Which people in your life might be asking those three questions about you right now? Make a list of names and write a short sentence as to why they might be asking.

What have you done recently to let those people know you care about them? What could you do *this week* to let a few more people know that you are *for* them?

Read Mark 10:35–45. In the New Testament, Jesus gives specific instructions throughout the Gospels on how to serve and love each other well. What does Jesus say about serving others?

How does the response Jesus gave to James and John apply to your life today?

Read Mark 12:28–30. Jesus said you love God by loving others— and in order to love others, you must love yourself. How does the way you love yourself reflect the way you love others?

Do you have a hard time or an easy time loving yourself? Do you have a hard or easy time loving others? Explain.

Spend a few moments reflecting on God's love. In what ways have you experienced it lately?

Is there an idea, quote, or passage of Scripture that inspires you to love and serve others? If so, write it here:

Close your time in prayer by thanking God for his love for you and the way he allows you to love yourself and serve the people around you. Ask him to give you opportunities this week to let your people know that you like them, you can help them, and they can trust you.

YOUR LIFE STRATEGY

Let's talk about your life strategy. According to the *Merriam-Webster Dictionary*, the word *strategy* means "a careful plan or method, or the art of devising or employing plans toward a goal."[3] Your life strategy is the way—the plan or method—that you live out your answers to the two key questions we discussed this week. Whether you want to admit it or not, you're already living out *some* kind of life strategy. But is it the one you really want to be living? Consider your life strategy as you answer the following questions:

What thoughts or questions come to mind when you think about having a life strategy?

Consider your daily routines and your weekly or monthly rhythms. How would you define what your life strategy has been until this point?

There are two vital components to a life strategy: your *purpose* and your *actions*. In fact, your life strategy is your purpose in action. How would you describe your specific purpose in life? What actions do you take to live out that purpose?

Now that you've identified what you're for and you've defined your purpose and your actions, revisit your life strategy. Where do you want your life strategy to be moving toward?

Your life strategy should easily translate to any environment where you are working, living, and serving. This is important because you don't just *tell* people you are for them but *show* them with your actions. Given this, how does your relationship with God influence your life strategy?

What keeps you from creating an intentional method or plan for your life? Are there any fears, past messages, or people holding you back from leaning into your life strategy?

Who could you share your life strategy with this week? Think of one or two people in your life who are safe and trustworthy—people who are *for* you. Write their names below.

If you're still kicking around a few life strategy ideas, ask for their input. What do they see as your life strategy? How would they describe your purpose and your actions?

Read Luke 6:43–44. In these verses, Jesus refers to the fruit in your life . . . and by *fruit*, he means your words and actions. Close your time in prayer today by thanking God for giving you the desire to produce good things from a good heart. Ask him to give you the willingness to consider the way he wants you to live out your life strategy.

FOR YOU

When you board a plane, every airline attendant says the same thing: "In case of an emergency, put your own oxygen mask on first." Life requires a lot of energy, creativity, and leadership, which means you need to spend time taking care of yourself so you can be the best version of you to give to others. Truly, the greatest gift you can give to the world around you is an inspired, rejuvenated, fully alive *you*. With this in mind, read Galatians 6:1–10. Use the space below to journal any thoughts, prayers, or ideas that come to mind as you read.

For Next Week: Review the Prologue and Introduction in the *Know What You're FOR* book and use the space below to write any insights or questions from your personal study that you want to discuss at the next group meeting. In preparation for next week, consider reviewing section one, chapters 1–7, in *Know What You're For.*

FOR YOUR WORLD

When you are known for one thing
but talk about being known for something else,
you lose an important value: credibility.

JEFF HENDERSON

WELCOME

It's easy to say we are *for* the people in our world, but would *they* say we're for *them*? We get sidetracked from time to time by whatever is going on in our own lives, and we forget we're a vital part of a larger story—that our words and actions actually have an impact on someone else's story. This is why I'm a big believer in visual cues that remind me of who and what I want to be *for* every day. I picked up this idea from the Notre Dame football team. Every time the players charge the field for a home game, they pass a sign on their way out of the locker room that reads, "Play Like a Champion Today." It's become a tradition for every player to tap it. Why? So they remember to *play like a champion* whenever they take the field.

One of my favorite stories about being *for* people comes from the time my wife and I stayed at the Ritz-Carlton to celebrate our tenth wedding anniversary. I knew from a previous trip that it was a hallmark of the hotel's customer service for the employees to call you by name the moment you stepped onto hotel property. The valet drivers would radio to the door holders and pass your name along when you arrived, so that everywhere you went, people would welcome you by name. Talk about being *for* someone!

But on our tenth wedding anniversary trip, when we checked into the hotel and walked to our room, we found ourselves standing outside the Presidential Suite. Surely, we thought, there had been a mistake. We are not really Presidential Suite kind of people . . . because our bank account isn't really a Presidential Suite kind of account. But low and behold, the key worked!

Later, when one of the hotel staff delivered a tray of chocolate-covered strawberries with a note mentioning our anniversary, we knew it was no mistake. They were *expecting* us to stay in the suite. But how? We read the note and found out a dear friend had remembered me saying something about staying at the Ritz-Carlton for our anniversary—and he surprised us with the upgrade. This friend was *for* us, and he made it known in a way that only he could do.

Now, we might not all be able to upgrade our friends, or our neighbors, or our colleagues to the Presidential Suite at the Ritz-Carlton. However, each of us *can* do something small that communicates we are for them. As my friend Andy Stanley says, we can all "do for one what we wish we could do for everyone."

SHARE

If you or any of your group members are just meeting for the first time, take a few minutes to introduce yourselves and share any insights you have from last week's personal study. Next, to kick things off for the group time, discuss one of the following questions:

- What has been one of the best gifts you've received from a friend?

— or —

- What reminders or visual cues do you keep to remind you to be *for* others?

WATCH

Play the video for session two. As you and your group watch, use the following outline to record any thoughts or key points that stand out to you.

Notes

When you are *for* the people in your world . . . the people in your life become *for* you. Imagine a world where employers are in favor of employees, churches are in favor of one another, and people strive to show they are in favor of each other.

Keep the main thing the main thing. Sometimes, if we're not careful, we can drift off of what is the main thing. When this happens, we lose our focus and the power of our message.

What is the *main thing* for God? We find the answer in a statement Jesus made to a man named Nicodemus in what has become arguably the most famous Bible verse of them all.

For God so loved the world that he gave his one and only Son, that whoever believes in him shall not perish but have eternal life.

JESUS (JOHN 3:16)

"For God . . ." These two words reveal that God is in favor of something. As people who represent God, this should be our calling card as well. Yes, there are things in this world we are

against, yet the power comes in demonstrating to others what we are in favor of.

"For God *so loved the world* . . ." These words reveal that God *emphatically* loves the people in the world. But even more, he loves each of us on a *personal* basis. God doesn't lose sight of us even in a planet filled with billions of other people.

If you think something is too small for God, your God is too small.

MARK BATTERSON

"For God so loved the world *that he gave his one and only Son . . .*" The value we place on something is seen by what we are willing to give up for it. God was willing to give up his only Son for us. The story of Jesus and our heavenly father is the price they paid on our behalf.

"For God so loved the world that he gave his one and only Son, *that whoever believes in him shall not perish but have eternal life.*" God gave his greatest possession for us—and the opportunity for us to have eternal life! Our response is simply to receive what God has provided.

God loved. God gave. We believe. We receive.

ANDY STANLEY

The message of the gospel is that God is *for* us. It's the message of the church . . . and we must make sure that we stay on message as we interact with others in our world.

DISCUSS

Take a few minutes with your group members to discuss what you just watched and explore these concepts together.

1. Have you ever had an unsuspecting moment when somebody showed what he or she was *for* to you? What was that experience like? How did it make you feel?

2. How do you know when people are *for* you? How have you witnessed this kind of favor shown to you at home, at work, at school, at church, or in your business?

3. The value that you place on something will be seen by what you're willing to give up for it. What have you had to give up recently because of what you value?

4. Read John 3:16–21. How did God demonstrate that he is *for* the people in the world? How should that impact the way you interact with others in your world?

5. How do you react to this idea that God truly is *for* you? What makes this concept easy or difficult for you to accept?

6. What can you do to begin to change the narrative so the people in your world know that God, the church, and you, are *for* them and not *against* them?

RESPOND

Briefly review the outline for the video teaching and any notes you took. In the space below, write down the most significant point you took away from this session.

What action step will you take this week to move toward what you want to be known *for*?

PRAY

End the gathering by praying together. If you are comfortable in doing so, share a vision or goal you are pursuing for your world this week. Pray that God would bring opportunities for you to show the people around you that God is *for* them . . . and so are you. Write down any specific requests in the space below so you can remember to continue praying throughout the week.

BETWEEN-SESSIONS
PERSONAL STUDY

The reality today is that many people are more familiar with what the church is *against* than what the church is *for*. This is why, as we discussed in this session, it is important for us to keep the main thing the main thing—and remember that God is for the people in the world. This week spend some time with God each day to explore this topic in the Bible as you engage in any or all of the following activities. Be sure to read the reflection questions and make a few notes that you can share at the next group meeting.

THE SPOTLIGHT

I'm often called in to consult with various organizations, and what I find time and time again is that people in the workplace have been taught to shine the spotlight on *themselves*—their organization, their services, their products, their accomplishments—and not the customer. Now, for this study, we can define *customer* as "others in the world around us." It's the people with whom we interact on a daily basis.

When we shine the spotlight on ourselves instead of "others in the world around us," it is what is called *narcissism*. I don't know about you, but I rarely find a person today who is comfortable with being labeled a narcissist. Yet that is what it is—and we need to be intentional and name it as such. We also need to be intentional about taking an honest look at ourselves to see if these self-focused tendencies exist so we can stamp out all forms of narcissism.

Horst Schulze, cofounder of the Ritz-Carlton, says the number one question our customers—those people in our world—are asking about us is, "Do they care?" They are not asking, "Do they care about themselves?" No, they want to know that we truly care about them. For this reason, we must learn to care about the interests of others more than our own self-interests. With this in mind, let's take a few moments to consider how we can shine the spotlight on others and let them know we are *for* them.

What is a bad customer service experience you had recently? Describe what happened.

Now recall a recent great customer service experience. What made it such a great experience?

What did it feel like to receive that kind of treatment from another person?

Who are your primary "customers"—the people in your world? What would they say about their "customer service experience" with you?

What can you do to shine the spotlight on these individuals? Write down some specific actions you can take to focus more on their needs than on your own.

Remember that God's spotlight is shining on *you* as a son or daughter in his world. What do you think God sees when he looks at his light shining on you?

Read Matthew 5:14–16. Jesus states in this passage that you are the light of the world—you are the one who represents him to the world around you—and you should never hide that light. Today, ask the Lord to show you new ways to reflect his love and mercy to those in the world. Pray that God will help others to know more and more each day that you are *for* them.

CREDIBILITY

Have you ever had a coworker, friend, or family member who made a lot of promises but did not follow through on them? This is not only frustrating but also exhausting. You end up working around that person, carrying extra responsibility because he or she failed to deliver, and questioning whether or not that person is really telling the truth.

As I mentioned in the first session, you lose credibility when you're *for* one thing but are *known for* something else. And once you lose credibility . . . you lose trust with people. This is why it is so important to close the gap between what you're *for* and what you're *known for.* When you're consistent, you will build credibility with the people around you. Consider what it looks like for you to have credibility in your world as you answer the following questions.

What does *credibility* mean to you? What words would you use to describe it?

What have you done to earn credibility with others?

How have you lost credibility with others?

In general, what kinds of actions and attitudes contribute to your credibility? What type of actions take away from your credibility?

How would you coach someone else to establish credibility—whether in business, a church, a community, a team, or in a family? What practices earn credibility?

It is important to also consider credibility from the perspective of the "customer," or the people in your world. From their perspective, what does it look like for you to have credibility with them?

When you consider your credibility through the eyes of others, it helps you *keep the main thing the main thing*—to be *for* those in your world. Do you think this is the perception others have of you? Why or why not?

What changes could you make to have greater credibility with others . . . and communicate that you are *for* them?

Read 1 John 5:1–12. Consider the credibility that Jesus had with the people of his day. When you put your trust in Jesus Christ, you have access to that same kind of credibility. So today, thank God for the gift of Jesus and the power of his presence in your life. Pray that God will help you to continue to steward that power for the goodness of others in the world.

THE MAIN THING

Have you ever visited a church or a business that has lost perspective on what it's like to be a guest in their environment? A friend was recently telling me about a coffee shop that gives off the vibe that customers show up just to annoy the employees. My friend was amazed to witness visible eyerolls when a customer ordered an item not found on the menu . . . which happens frequently, because the menu is on a piece of paper tucked out of sight.

I also think about churches that don't have signs telling visitors where to drop off their children for kids ministry or how to get into the worship center. These organizations have what I call a case of *insideritis*. They cater to their "members" at the exclusion of others. If we're not careful, we can develop insideritis as well. When all we do is advocate for our own interests or what's best for our family without considering others, we've caught the insideritis bug.

The antidote to insideritis is *keeping the main thing the main thing*. How do you do this? By focusing on the following four areas:

- **What you see:** keep the vision visible
- **What you celebrate:** catch people doing right
- **Where you meet**: get out of the office
- **What you talk about:** discuss what's helpful for others

Keep these points in mind as you use the following questions to determine how to keep the main thing the main thing in your life. As you answer these questions, reflect on one specific area—your home, your business, your church community, *or* on your life as a whole.

What do you currently do to get an outside perspective? How do you push against *insideritis*?

What is the main thing you want to keep as the main thing in your life?

What do people see when they look at your life? What are the visual cues that tell others who and what you're *for*?

What do you celebrate—as an organization, a family, or an individual?

What stories do you tell about your celebration experiences?

How do you find your stories to celebrate? Is there a system or a rhythm (like a team meeting, family dinner time, or weekly coffee with a friend) that helps you to find these stories? Explain.

What do you spend your time talking about the most? Is the topic most often about yourself or your organization, or is it about others? Explain.

Think about the groups of which you are a part—whether at work, at your church, or in your family. How is what you talk about the most when you're together helping the people you are trying to serve?

Read Romans 5:6–11. Consider what the apostle Paul writes is the *main thing* of the gospel message: *the great love of God through the sacrifice of Jesus.* Ask God to help you keep this message in perspective as you seek to serve others and keep your main thing the main thing.

FOR YOU

We've talked a lot about being *for* others in this study. But the truth is when we choose people, they choose us. When we are *for* others, they become *for* us. Of course, we need to watch our motives here. We can't be *for* others just so they're *for* us. But the great benefit of being *for* others is that most often they become *for* us too. Hear the difference between the two?

When I worked at Chick-fil-A, I often encountered customers who were "raving fans." These were the people who showed up more often to our restaurants, paid full price, and told other customers about us. They generated positive word-of-mouth and drew other people into our restaurants . . . who could, in turn, also become raving fans for the company.

In our lives, when the people around us become a "raving fan" of our working relationship, our friendship, our family environment, or our community engagement, they become *for* us. They show up and support us, listen to us, and hang with us through tough seasons. This begins by authentically engaging with people in the world around us—by letting them know we *see them*, *celebrate them*, and are *there for them*. With this in mind, read Romans 8:31–39. As you meditate on this passage, use the space below to journal any thoughts, prayers or ideas that come to mind.

For Next Week: Use the space below to write any key insights or questions from your personal study that you want to discuss at the next group meeting. In preparation for next week, consider reviewing section two, chapters 8–14, in the *Know What You're For* book.

FOR YOUR TEAM

When you spend eight hours a day, five days a week with people, they become more than a team. It's somewhere between team and family. We celebrate together. We holler at one another. We encourage each other. It's just like family.

SID MASHBURN

WELCOME

I have a friend who keeps a folder of the kind notes she receives from others. She calls this her "encouragement folder" because it is filled with notes of gratitude and encouraging words from colleagues, friends, family members—and occasionally random strangers. When she is having a bad day at work or she is in a hard season, my friend pulls out one of these notes and reads it to herself. She doesn't go parading the notes around the office—she just quietly keeps them to herself when she needs a shot of encouragement.

I have another friend who worked for a consulting firm doing organizational development. Every year, the owner would pull the team together in early November for a signing party. Each partner, consultant, and operations member would clear their calendars and spend the day in the board room passing cards around the table. They would order take-out for lunch, make some extra coffee, and use the time to catch up with each other while signing the cards. The owner of the firm thought it was more impactful for their clients and colleagues to receive a hand-signed note of appreciation from the team around the Thanksgiving holiday than to receive the standard auto-stamped Christmas card. This was the best way they knew how to show their customers they were *for* them.

Another friend starts off each staff development conversation he has with those on his team by asking how they are doing personally. He said it took some time before all the team members were willing to share some of their personal lives with him. In fact, he often had to go first by giving them a quick update on his own personal life. But eventually this kind of conversation developed into a rhythm and became the norm for the organization. This is the kind of conversation that communicated they were *for* one another.

I cannot tell you how meaningful it is to express appreciation to the people in your life with a simple handwritten note, or by asking good questions, or by actually listening to the answers. This goes a long way in building *trust*—what I think is one of the key elements to success in business and in life. When you take the time to build trust with the people around you, you communicate you care more about being *for* them than what you want from them.

SHARE

Begin your group time by inviting anyone to share his or her insights from last week's personal study. Next, to kick things off, discuss one of the following questions:

- What are some of the ways you have felt appreciated by someone else?

— *or* —

- What is one question you wish someone—your boss, your coach, your team, your family, your friends, or your pastor—would ask you? Why?

WATCH

Play the video for session three. As you and your group watch, use the following outline to record any thoughts or key points that stand out to you.

Notes

Sometimes, our character and our success will seem to be on opposite sides. However, as we read in Proverbs 22:1, "a good name is to be chosen rather than great riches" (ESV).

Most people can bear adversity; but if you wish to know what a man really is give him power. This is the supreme test.

ROBERT G. INGERSOLL

All of us have decisions about who we will ultimately stand for and who we will be. Developing a for-the-team strategy will not only help us build an amazing culture in our workplace, family, or ministry but will also help us to develop the character *we* want to have in life.

The first way to develop a for-the-team strategy is to *believe abundantly*. Thriving businesses, families, and marriages all have a culture in which they believe the best about one another. They not only *believe* this . . . but they also *communicate* it to one another.

> ## Unexpressed gratitude communicates ingratitude.
>
> ANDY STANLEY

The second way to develop a for-the-team strategy is to *appreciate consistently*. One of the best ways we can do this is by giving handwritten notes of encouragement to those on our team and in our world. This tells those in our relationships that we are truly for them.

The third way to develop a for-the-team strategy is to *develop intentionally*—or what I call "become a big *L* leader." A big *L* leader is growing in three areas of leadership:

Thought leadership

People leadership

Project leadership

One of the most effective ways to grow the organization is to grow the people in the organization.

JEFF HENDERSON

The fourth way to develop a for-the-team strategy is to *listen actively*. There are three primary steps we can take to actively listen to others:

Ask great questions—"tell me more . . ."

Listen for insights

Act on what we hear

The fifth way to develop a for-the-team strategy is to *live it repeatedly*. Vision rarely repeated is quickly forgotten. For this reason, we have to put our vision on repeat, say it over and over again, and live it out repeatedly in front of others.

DISCUSS

Take a few minutes with your group members to discuss what you just watched and explore these concepts together.

1. Who is someone in your life who *believed abundantly* in you? What did that person do to communicate his or her support and belief in you?

2. What does it look like for you to *appreciate consistently*? What are some ways that you show your appreciation to others on a regular and consistent basis?

3. Who is someone in your life whom you admire as a "big *L* leader"? What does that person do to communicate his or her vision to you?

4. What is the value of *listening actively* to the people on our "team"—whether that is in our work, in our families, or in our friendships? How does active listening demonstrate humility on our part and show we value the other person's ideas?

5. Why is it critical to *live out your vision repeatedly* for those in your world?

6. Read Mark 10:46–52. How did Jesus demonstrate that he valued Bartimaeus?

RESPOND

Briefly review the outline for the video teaching and any notes you took. In the space below, write down the most significant point you took away from this session.

What action step will you take this week to move toward being *for* the people on your "team"?

PRAY

End the gathering by praying for each other. Pray especially that God would help you contribute to the growth of the relationships around you as you serve your team, your friends, your family, and your community. Write down any specific requests in the space below so you can remember to continue praying throughout the week.

What action step will you take this week to move toward what you want to be known *for*?

BETWEEN-SESSIONS
PERSONAL STUDY

We talked in this session about what it means to build a for-the-team strategy. Regardless of your work situation or where you are in life, I hope you can see the various "teams" you have—whether that is your family, your roommates, your staff, a group of close friends, your small group at church, or your neighborhood. For most of us, these are simply called *relationships*. For the sake of this personal study, you can either keep a specific "team" in mind or consider a broad perspective of the various relationships in your life. Either way works as long as you're willing to be specific with your answers to the questions. As always, be sure to make a few notes as you do your personal study that you can share at the next group meeting.

LEAVING A LEGACY

Truett Cathy died in September 2014. As I reflected on his life, I realized I wanted to leave a legacy like him . . . or a legacy like my friends Sid and Ann Mashburn. Sid and Ann are married entrepreneurs who own and operate an independent clothing store.[4] She sells women's clothing, and he sells men's clothing. What I love about Sid and Ann isn't that they're super successful—in fact, success is just a side note to them. I love that Sid and Ann see their roles as shop owners and retailers as *taking care of people*.

Sid and Ann's mission in life is to provide *hopefulness* and *helpfulness* each and every day—first to their team, and then to their customers. This is exactly what they do. They say, "A question we ask ourselves is, *How do we enhance someone's life?* We believe hopefulness and helpfulness is the way. This isn't a business philosophy; it's a life philosophy." I would add that it's also the legacy that they are leaving behind. Keeping this example in mind, consider your legacy that you are leaving behind as you reflect on the following questions.

How would you define the word "legacy"? What does it mean to you?

Now, go back to previous sessions where you defined your answers to the following questions. Rewrite your answers in the space below:

What are you for?

What do you *want* to be known for?

What is your life strategy (purpose + actions = strategy)?

What kind of legacy do you want to leave behind? What do you hope people say about you someday?

As we learn from Ann and Sid Mashburn, people are drawn to humility when it is displayed in the workplace. The same is true with kindness, hopefulness, and helpfulness. These are the "soft skills" that can make all the difference in our success in the workplace, in our career, and in our lives. What soft skills are you known for in your relationships?

How have your soft skills contributed to making a difference in the lives of others?

What soft skills do you admire most in your colleagues, your family members, your friends, and your neighbors? (Take a few moments this week to send a text, write a note, or let them know face to face what you admire most about the way they show up in the world.)

Read John 4:1–42. In this story, Jesus gives the Samaritan woman at the well a chance to redefine her legacy. In essence, it's as though he's saying, "Your past doesn't define who you have the potential to become today." As we trust in Jesus, he gives us the opportunity to leave a new legacy if we pay attention to him and to the relationships he's placed around us. So close today by thanking God for his legacy through Jesus. And thank God for giving you the opportunity to leave the kind of legacy that makes a difference in your relationships.

DESIGNING A *FOR* CULTURE

We create a culture by default or design. We can either be intentional about it and shape our culture, or we can just allow it to happen by default. Now, this is not to say we can dictate every square inch of what happens in our lives, but we *can* set a healthy framework for everyone to follow. In my life, when my kids are clear on the house rules, there is less confusion, more clarity, and more creativity. My kids are not waiting for me to give orders, because they know what's expected. They also have the freedom to bring their perspective to what's expected.

The same is true when you create a framework for your "team"—for the people in your work, in your family, in your friendships, and in your community. Remember the five principles we discussed of designing a for-the-team culture:

1. Believe abundantly
2. Appreciate consistently
3. Develop intentionally
4. Listen actively
5. Live repeatedly

Consider a particular team of which you are a part as you respond to the following questions.

What does it feel like to be part of that team? What are some of the characteristics of the team that you like and don't like?

What does it feel like to do business there—or engage in relationships there?

Do the members of the team believe in each other? If so, how do they show it?

Do the members of the team appreciate one other? If so, how do they express it?

Do the members of the team develop one another? If so, how do they do this?

Do the members of the team listen actively to one another? If so, what are some ways this can be further fostered and encouraged?

Do the members of the team have a vision for what they are doing? If so, how are they living out that vision repeatedly?

If you answered no to any of these questions, what kind of changes need to be made in the culture—whether at work, at home, at church, or in your community?

Read John 15:9–17. In this passage, we see that Jesus developed a for-the-team culture long before we arrived on the scene. Here he breaks down the barrier between master and servant by calling those who love him *friends*. Today, consider what it's like to have Jesus as a true friend—someone who is *for* you. Thank God for the gift of Jesus and for the love he so freely gives to you. Ask God to show you what it's like to truly love your co-workers, teammates, classmates, friends, neighbors, and family with this kind of love.

LISTEN ACTIVELY

Remember that the fourth principle we discussed is *listen actively*. Now, you might be saying, "I know how to listen!" But do you know how to listen *actively*? My experience is that this kind of listening takes a little practice. As I stated, this kind of listening is captured by the example of Cheryl Bachelder, who went on a "listening tour" to really find out what were the issues at Popeye's Louisiana Chicken.[5] It involves:

- Asking great questions
- Listening for insights
- Acting on what you hear

When done correctly, this kind of listening communicates to other people that *you see them, you hear them, you value their opinion,* and *you want to learn more.* With this in mind, consider the following questions about how you can grow in the skill of active listening.

What do you see as the difference between listening and listening actively?

Think about a time when someone listened actively to you. What was that experience like?

The first component of listening actively is asking great questions. How would you define or explain great questions?

The second component is listening for insights. What does it look like to do this well?

The third component is acting on what you hear. What does this look like? Can you think of someone who does this well?

How will you put these active listening skills to use this week? Be specific.

Do you need to act on something you have already heard from your team? If so, what is it? When will you do it?

Listening actively often leads to innovation. Can you think of a time when you changed course because of someone else's innovative answer? What happened?

Read Mark 5:24–34. Consider what might have happened to the woman if she had not been persistent in seeking healing—or if Jesus had not been persistent in finding her. Active listening requires persistence, and while it might seem to be a difficult task for us, Jesus is no stranger to persistence. So ask God today to give you opportunities to practice listening actively. Be persistent in your pursuit of those opportunities for the good of the relationships in your life. Also thank God for the way he listens actively and responds to you.

FOR YOU

One key lesson I've learned about leadership development is this: *You cannot intentionally develop the people around you unless you're willing to intentionally develop yourself.* The same goes with friendships, working relationships, and family relationships. You cannot develop those relationships unless you're willing to work on how you show up in those relationships.

Earlier, I mentioned there are three ways to intentionally develop others: (1) by being a *thought leader,* (2) by being a *people leader,* and (3) by being a *project leader.* As individuals grow in these three areas, they grow into what my friend David Farmer calls a "Big *L* Leader," and move closer to their potential.[6] You can apply these three areas to your life as well.

Take a few moments to consider the ways you are intentionally developing yourself in these areas. It may be tempting for your mind to drift toward how you're developing others, but the focus here is you. This is *for you.*

Thought Leader: How do you see the future of your business, your family, your classroom, your church, or your community? How are you shaping that future?

People Leader: Are you growing? Is your team growing? How would you describe the growth that is taking place?

Project Leader: How can you be more effective and efficient with your time and energy?

Read Jeremiah 17:7–8 for your personal reflection this week. As you meditate on this passage, use the space below to journal any thoughts, prayers, or ideas that come to mind.

For Next Week: Use the space below to write any key insights or questions from your personal study that you want to discuss at the next group meeting. In preparation for next week, consider reviewing section three, chapters 15–17, in the *Know What You're For* book.

FOR YOUR COMMUNITY

If your church closed down, would the community even notice? Don't forget, people are searching for a community to which they can belong. Not just a physical neighborhood—but something deeper and even more tangible that will meet this need to belong.

JEFF HENDERSON

WELCOME

I know a guy who recently bought a Harley-Davidson motor-cycle. As soon as he finished signing the paperwork, he was handed the keys and ushered outside to meet his new ride. He hopped on the bike, snapped the helmet around his chin, revved the engine, and looked up to see the Harley employees had formed two lines in front of him on either side of the dealership driveway. As he drove away, the employees clapped and cheered in celebration.

You can bet that in this moment that guy was feeling like a million bucks. Then, a few days later, he was invited to a party hosted by the dealership so he could meet the rest of the "tribe"—other riders who belonged to the "Harley Nation." For Harley-Davidson, the purchase of a motorcycle is bigger than the bike. It's about belonging to a greater community and the deep sense of personal freedom that comes with owning one of their motorcycles.

Can you imagine buying something from your favorite store and receiving a standing ovation on the way out? I'm guessing you would feel pretty good about yourself in that moment. Or, if you prefer to shop online, imagine a flower delivery or your favorite pizza showing up at your door minutes after you finalized a purchase. It sounds over the top—yet businesses today are going to great lengths to welcome consumers into their *community*. These businesses want us to know they are *for* us—not only as customers, but also as people.

So, what if we leaned into this mindset in our churches? What if we became a source of encouragement, support, and personal freedom for our communities—and in so doing, also became a place of belonging? Some of us think we're doing this really well, but I'm not sure our communities would agree. It's the gap we've been talking about between what we *want* to be for and what we're *actually* known for. If we really want our communities to know that we're *for* them, we have to do our part to pay attention to their needs.

It's important for those of us who are in the church to create a sense of belonging by providing real encouragement and support—the kind that celebrates the members of our community, not just the members of our church. And, as we will see in this session, both Jesus and the apostle Paul actually gave us a pattern to follow when it comes to being *for* our communities.

SHARE

Begin your group time by inviting anyone to share his or her insights from last week's personal study. Next, to kick things off, discuss one of the following questions:

- What symbols or logos stand out most to you? Why?

— or —

- Have you ever purchased something from a store and were instantly made to feel like you were part of their community? Briefly share your experience.

WATCH

Play the video for session four. As you and your group watch, use the following outline to record any thoughts or key points that stand out to you.

Notes

The Coca-Cola logo is the second most recognizable symbol in the world. The first is the *cross*. We in the church have work to do in explaining the meaning, invitation, and power of the cross—not just in the world but also in our communities.

Many people have said *no* to Jesus, the church, and what we believe. How do we respond to this? Jesus gives us an example to follow in Luke 19:1–10 in an interaction he had with a man named Zacchaeus, who climbed a sycamore-fig tree one day to see Christ.

> Zacchaeus' action: "He wanted to see who Jesus was . . . so he ran ahead and climbed a sycamore-fig tree" (verses 3–4).

Jesus' response: "Zacchaeus, come down immediately. I must stay at your house today" (verse 5).

The people's response: "He has gone to be the guest of a sinner" (verse 7).

Zacchaeus' response: "Look, Lord! Here and now I give half of my possessions to the poor, and if I have cheated anybody out of anything, I will pay back four times the amount" (verse 8).

Jesus' reaction: "Today, salvation has come to this house, because this man, too, is a son of Abraham. For the Son of Man came to seek and to save the lost" (verses 9–10).

Jesus made it clear that he has come to seek and save *the lost*. The term implies value—the lost are valuable to Jesus. Given this, shouldn't they be valuable to us as well?

> ## The reason many people have said no to Jesus is because they feel like his church has said no to them.
>
> JEFF HENDERSON

To reach the lost and show we are *for* them, we need to push back against *insider thinking*. Our mission—like that of Jesus— must be focused on seeking and saving the lost.

How do we begin to say yes to those who have said no to Christ so we can seek and save the lost? In Acts 17:16–23, we read of an interaction Paul had with a group of philosophers in the city of Athens. His example provides us with two steps we can follow:

> First, we say yes by *listening* and *observing*. "[Paul] was greatly distressed to see that the city was full of idols. So he reasoned in the synagogue with both Jews and

God-fearing Greeks, as well as in the marketplace day by day" (verses 16–17).

Second, we say yes by asking *how we can help.* "[Paul said], 'As I walked around and looked carefully at your objects of worship, I even found an altar with this inscription: TO AN UNKNOWN GOD. So you are ignorant of the very thing you worship—and this is what I am going to proclaim to you'" (verses 22–23).

Do for one what you wish you could do for everyone.

ANDY STANLEY

There needs to be a common language in our churches that communicate a purpose that can be understood by both those inside and outside the church. This is why the *for*

language is so important. It builds a common language and
bond, because it says we are for this community.

DISCUSS

Take a few minutes with your group members to discuss what
you just watched and explore these concepts together.

1. What comes to mind when you think about the cross as
   a symbol for the Christian faith and for the church?

2. Have you or someone you know ever said *no* to
   Jesus because of an experience with the church?
   Briefly explain.

3. How have you responded to people who have said *no* to the church? How have those people responded back to you?

4. What can you do to show those who are far from God and far from the church that Jesus is actually *for* them? How is your church making your community better?

5. Reread Luke 19:1–10. What stands out about the interaction between Jesus and Zacchaeus? Is there a modern-day Zacchaeus in your life who you need to notice?

6. How can you *"do for one what you wish you could do for everyone"* this week as you pay attention to your community and follow the pattern of Jesus?

RESPOND

Briefly review the outline for the video teaching and any notes you took. In the space below, write down the most significant point you took away from this session.

What action will you take this week to move toward what you want the church to be known for in your community?

PRAY

End the gathering by briefly sharing the name of a person or group of people to whom you want to pray for this week. Pray that God would help the person or group see that Jesus and the church are *for* them through your invitation. Write down any specific requests in the space below so you can remember to continue praying throughout the week.

BETWEEN-SESSIONS
PERSONAL STUDY

The world is looking for organizations that want to make people's lives better and our earth a better place to live. From my perspective, that sounds like a great opportunity for the church. But are we truly making that kind of difference in our communities? Are people in the world noticing us for what we are doing for our neighborhoods? Or would the community even notice if we shut our doors one day and closed down the church? Asking these kinds of questions creates a reality check—not just for pastors and leaders in the church, but for laypeople and members of the community as well. As you work through these personal study exercises this week, take a few moments to reflect on how your church shows up in your community. As always, be sure to make a few notes that you can share at the next group meeting.

FOR YOUR COMMUNITY

When we talk about the church creating a place for people to *belong,* we're actually talking about a fundamental human need—the need to be a part of something bigger than ourselves. People today aren't just searching for a *physical* community but something deeper and even more tangible.

When we ignore this basic human need, we overlook the opportunity to impact the people in our world . . . and ultimately present to them the gospel of Christ.

Belonging is one of those intangible qualities that is hard to measure but it has a powerful impact on the mission of every church. When we understand the power of belonging, we are able to take our message into the wider community and, at the same time, provide an anchor for our own members. *Belonging* is what holds it all together. With that in mind, consider the purpose of your church in the community as you answer the following questions.

What problem is your church or ministry trying to solve for the community?

How are you making your community better?

To what larger purpose do the members of your church or ministry believe they belong?

What would your church or ministry *like* to be known for in the community?

What do you believe your church or ministry *is* known for in the community?

What are you doing for the good of others—with no strings attached?

Read Matthew 22:34–40. In this passage, Jesus gives his followers "the great commandment," which should guide not only the way we live but also the way we show up in our community. Close today by asking God to give you new perspective on your community. Ask God to reveal how you can be a church *for* your community in tangible ways. Thank God for the sense of belonging in which he invites us to participate in his kingdom community here on earth.

YOUR RESPONSE

The first thing people will sense as they walk through the doors of your church is your congregation's *response* to them. Are they warm and inviting? Are they helpful about what's going on? If not, you will miss out on an opportunity to make a great first impression. Yet this isn't the goal—the goal is to create a sense of community . . . a place where people feel they can *belong*. In the case of Gwinnett Church, we have opportunities to make a first impression with our community *before* anyone ever steps a foot inside our church doors.

So let's consider some ways your church can respond to the people in your community so as to communicate they *belong* in your church. Now, if you're not part of a traditional church, that is okay. You can substitute the word *church* for whatever place describes where you *belong*. Consider your answers to the following questions on behalf of your neighborhood, organization, business, family, or group of friends:

What was it like for you to attend your church for the first time? What do you remember about that experience?

What is it about your church that gives you a sense of belonging?

What is the "word on the street" about your church? (If you're not sure, it's okay to ask someone in your community, *"What's your impression of us?"*)

Do you think people in your community see your church as *for* them or *against* them? Give some reasons and examples for why you believe this way.

How does your church respond to guests? What do you do to create a safe space for people to belong *even before they believe?*

What could your church do to improve the way you respond to guests or those who consider themselves "outsiders"? Is there a system for providing this kind of feedback to the leadership? (If so, consider offering your suggestions.)

Are there other churches or organizations in your community already creating a strong sense of belonging? If so, what can you learn from them?

Read Acts 15:1–11. In this passage, Paul and Barnabas are in a debate with a group who held that believers had to be circumcised and follow Old Testament law in order to be considered Christians. This debate is essentially about the Jewish believers' response to the Gentile believers and what it means for them to *belong* to the church community. Today, close by asking God to reveal how you can influence the way your church responds to your community. Ask the Lord to continue to show you ways to extend that sense of belonging in your community, regardless of whether people ever walk through the doors of your church. Above all else, pray that the people in your community would find their belonging in God.

HOW CAN WE HELP?

The better you know the community surrounding your church, the better your church can serve the surrounding community. One of the best ways to do this is to get *curious* about your community. Whether the doors of your church have been open for six months or twenty years, it's never too late to search for problems you can help solve. However, for this to occur, you have to be curious and ask the question, "How can we help?"

This is a great question to ask the mayor or city officials. It's a great question to ask any community organizers with whom you connect. And it's a great question to ask your neighbors. The point of asking this question is that you want your impact to flow well beyond the physical and virtual walls of your church. You want to add value to people's lives—not just *spiritual* value, but tangible, practical, physical value to the community.

Here are three practical ways you can add value to your community:

- Listen to people in your community.
- Talk with people in your community.
- Celebrate the people in your community.

Sounds simple . . . and it is. The difficult part is just putting it into action. So consider ways your church can add value to your community as you answer these questions.

How well are you listening to people in your community?

What spaces and places are you spending time in as you listen? (This could include physical spaces like the local grocery store or corner coffee shop or digital spaces like the hashtag for your community or social media accounts.)

Would your community say that your church and its members are listening to them? Why or why not?

How well do you feel that are you talking with the people in your community?

Where are you showing up for these conversations?

What kinds of questions are you asking? How are you staying curious about your community?

How does your presence in the community "humanize" your church and its purpose?

What are you doing to celebrate your community? What kind of input from those in your community do you gather to plan your celebrations?

Read Hebrews 10:24–25. Consider how you might influence and encourage your community with love and good deeds. Close by asking God to show you a few specific areas where your church could make an impact and what your specific involvement should be. Remember God is with you every step of the way. He is *for* you and *for* your community!

FOR YOU

In the beginning of this section, we raised the question as to whether people in the community would even notice if most churches closed their doors. I think there's a personal application here as well. Consider the way you show up in your community—your church, your neighborhood, and the places where you work and serve. If you disappeared, would people notice? Would they call you or text you and ask where you were?

Maybe there's an element of loneliness in your life right now that makes these questions hard to consider. If that's the case, then I am sorry this is such a challenging season for you. My prayer for you is that you will find a deep sense of belonging in a healthy and vibrant community where you have the opportunity to live out your potential. But what I want to do here is encourage you to *show up* in your community in the best way you know how—so that if you were absent, people *would* notice.

Here's an example of what I mean. Let's say a few streets over from your house, there is a kid who rides his scooter up and down the sidewalk every day after school. Occasionally he rings the doorbell of a neighbor to say hello or pet their dog. He knowns the name of almost every single person on the block. When this kid goes out of town, his neighbors notice. Why? Because this kid is *present* in the community.

He is there. People regard him as a member of their neighborhood, so they feel his absence when he is not there.

With this in mind, read James 5:13–20. As you meditate on this passage, use the space below to journal any thoughts, prayers, or ideas that come to mind.

For Next Week: Use the space below to write any key insights or questions from your personal study that you want to discuss at the next group meeting. In preparation for next week, consider reviewing section four, chapters 18–19, and the Epilogue in the *Know What You're For* book.

FOR YOUR LIFE

Success is measuring yourself against other people. Excellence is measuring yourself against your own potential. When you choose excellence, you move closer to your potential.

TIM TASSOPOULOS

WELCOME

Have you ever wanted something so badly that you have been afraid to say it out loud because you feared your request wouldn't be granted? *Me too.*

As you watch this final session, you will hear about my Pixar story. It has a happy ending, of course, because I want to encourage you with the big asks in your own life. But the truth is I could have had a million other moments like the Pixar story—if only I had asked boldly or dreamed big early on in my life. Instead, I spent many years saying *no* to my own requests and dreams and never gave anyone the opportunity to say *yes* to me.

I am sure you can relate. Settling for second just seems to be a human thing. But I want you to think about *why* we so often say no to ourselves on behalf of others. What keeps us from asking boldly or dreaming big? For some of us, it's fear. We're afraid to ask because we don't want to be told no. For others, it's history. We've asked boldly and dreamed big in the past only to be shut down. Or maybe it's due to failure, or because you lost your creative inspiration along the way. You don't remember what it feels like, sounds like, or looks like to be bold and dream big. So you trudge along and keep on doing what you're doing. You have a pulse that keeps you alive, but you've lost the spring in your step and the light in your eyes.

When I get to this place—as I have many times before—I always wonder if this is really the life God has for me to live. God's response to me in those prayerful moments of wondering has always been simple and clear: *remain in me.* So, here's how I want to encourage you today. God, the author of life and creator of the Universe, wants you to live a life full of creativity, passion, and purpose. But God wants you to *want* to live this kind of life. God wants you to dream big, ask boldly, seek answers, and live the life that he has for you.

Finding this life requires staying connected to Jesus. In Jesus, you will find the strength and courage to keep dreaming, keep seeking, and keep asking as you live *for* God, *for* your world, *for* your relationships, and *for* your community.

SHARE

Begin your group time by inviting anyone to share his or her insights from last week's personal study. Next, to kick things off, discuss one of the following questions:

- Have you ever made a "big ask" that was granted? If so, what happened?

  — *or* —

- Have you experienced the death of a dream? What was that like for you?

WATCH

Play the video for session five. As you and your group watch, use the following outline to record any thoughts or key points that stand out to you.

Notes

One of the best ways that you can be for your customer, your team, your family, your community is by giving them an inspired, healthy you. And one of the best ways to fight for them and to be for them is to fight and be for you.

There is a command from Scripture that we might refer to as *the bold ask*. In Romans 8:31, Paul says, "If God is for us, who can be against us?" In other words, if God is for us . . . let's act like it. Let's ask boldly, dream boldly, and remain inspired by the reality that God is for us.

If your future vision outpaces your current resources, you're on the right track.

JEFF HENDERSON

Jesus encourages us to make the big ask in Matthew 7:7-9. Many of us approach this passage hesitantly, because we have been disappointed in the past when we made "the big ask." This raises the question: Is Jesus over-promising and under-delivering in this passage?

This passage is not about faith but about *obedience*. Our responsibility is to ask, seek, and knock. God's responsibility is to give, find, and open. Seeing *ask* as an act of obedience can help us to stay more persistent in asking boldly in prayer.

There is a pattern with every idea or dream. There is the *birth* of the idea, the *death* of the idea, the *resurrection* of the idea, and the *ascension* of the idea. When you have an idea, you have to move through the death of the idea so that you can see it resurrected.

Jesus is asking us to remain obedient even when it seems like the dream dies—to believe that God is for us and no one can stand against us. There are three ways we remain obedient:

(1) keep inspired, (2) remain in the land of possibility, and (3) stay connected to Jesus.

We don't deny reality. We don't deny that dreams sometimes die. But neither do we let the reality define us. We are possibility people.

JEFF HENDERSON

Let's start seeking again. Let's start knocking again. Let's do our part, and then let Jesus do his part. The reason why this is so important is because sometimes we do get a *yes*. But we will never get a *yes* until we ask. So be obedient to the bold ask. After all, God is *for* you.

DISCUSS

Take a few minutes with your group members to discuss what you just watched and explore these concepts together.

1. Think about *what kind of life is flowing from you*. What are your dreams, goals, and ambitions? In what ways are you fighting to make those things a reality?

2. Do you believe that even *when your dream dies, God is still for you*? Why or why not? How would you answer that question in regard to the death of one of your dreams?

3. Have you stopped asking boldly when it comes to your hopes and dreams? If so, why do you think these hopes and dreams are not as big or bold as they once were?

4. How does it help you to see Jesus' command to "ask, seek, knock" as an act of obedience rather than an act of faith? How does that change your perspective?

5. Read John 15:1–16. What does Jesus say about himself as the "vine"? What happens when you remain in him? How can you let Jesus do his part in your life?

6. How can others encourage you to live the life God has for you? What encouragement do you need from the rest of the group so you can ask boldly and pursue your dreams?

RESPOND

Briefly review the outline for the video teaching and any notes you took. In the space below, write down the most significant point you took away from this session.

What action step will you take this week to move toward living the life God has *for* you?

PRAY

End the gathering by praying for one another. Pray especially that God would help you ask boldly, dream big, and remain in him regardless of the outcomes in your life. Pray for courage to live the life God has for you as individuals and as a community. Write down any requests in the space below so you can remember to continue praying throughout the week.

BETWEEN-SESSIONS
PERSONAL STUDY

When people say they lack purpose, it's often because they're unsure of their purpose. This is why I believe in the two key questions we've been asking: (1) *What are you for?* and (2) *What are you known for?* When you can answer those two questions, you will be on your way to defining your purpose. It also helps to have a life verse that reminds you of your purpose—such as the one Truett Cathy had: "A good name is to be chosen rather than great riches" (Proverbs 22:1 ESV). When you decide what you want to be known *for,* this passage can guide your every decision and every action. Talk about a powerful strategy for life! With this in mind, spend time with God each day to explore this topic of purpose as you engage in the following activities.

LIVING UP TO YOUR POTENTIAL

I like to learn from friends and mentors who are living their best lives because I'm curious about their secrets for success. I used to have a favorite question to ask these individuals: "What's your definition of success?" But a few years ago, one such friend told me I was asking the wrong question. Tim challenged me to ask a different question—a question about potential.

All too often, we spend our days comparing ourselves to other people in a feeble attempt to measure our success. But if we're willing to let go of our idea of success and focus on our *potential*, our growth fosters a greater impact for others. Growth and potential go hand in hand. So, now my question sounds more like, "How are you moving closer to your potential?" You would be amazed at the rich responses I hear from people all over the place. Consider how your growth contributes to your own potential as you answer these questions.

How would you define the word *potential*? Do you think you're living up to your potential? Briefly describe why or why not.

In what ways are you pursuing personal growth to reach your potential?

What happens when you feel stuck or uninspired? How do you keep moving forward?

What does it look like to be the healthy and inspired version of you? What does it look like to be the unhealthy, uninspired version of you?

What kind of emotional and relational climate do you create in a room full of people?

How would others describe the kind of life that flows out of you?

Read Ephesians 3:14–20. In this passage, Paul refers to the potential he sees in the congregation in Ephesus because of God's work in their lives. We have access to the same power and the same potential as followers of Jesus! So today, ask God to help you remember to rely on his strength as you pursue personal growth and your full potential. Thank God for the invitation to lean into your potential as you live the life he has *for* you.

THE PATTERN OF LIFE

I wish we had time to grab a cup of coffee and talk about our big *asks*—those moments where we asked for something outrageous (like my private tour of Pixar) and those dreams came true. I imagine we would all have some crazy stories to share. But I also wonder about the times when we've experienced the death of an idea or the loss of a dream. In fact, for many of us, we may not have any "big ask" stories because we're trying to avoid the painful "what-ifs":

- *What if they say no?*
- *What if it doesn't turn out the way I hope?*
- *What if I'm not good enough?*
- *What if I fail . . . again?*

I am sure you could fill in your own "what-if" statement. But there is something helpful we can learn from the life of Jesus to help us move past these what-ifs and our fears: *everything in life has a pattern.* Think of the pattern this way as it relates to an idea (or our big asks). Most of our ideas go through each one of these stages: (1) the *birth* of the idea, (2) the *death* of the idea, (3) the *resurrection* of the idea, and (4) the *ascension* of the idea. However, we have to stay the course to see our idea through to the end—just like we have to remain obedient in living the life God has for us if we want to experience that best life.

I don't know about you, but I'm often tempted to do my own thing after the death of one of my ideas. Rarely do I have the willpower to remain obedient and stay the course to the point where I get to experience the resurrection and ascension of anything at all. But I know that if I choose to *remain* in God, then I get to experience the full cycle of the pattern. I get to experience the delight of my ideas and big asks. Today, consider what this pattern looks like in your own life as you answer the following questions.

What ideas (or big asks) have recently been birthed in you?

What are you doing to contribute to the birth of those ideas? How do you create space for those ideas to come into existence?

What ideas have recently died? What ideas are losing momentum?

Do you remember a time when one of your ideas was resurrected? How did this idea come back to life?

What was that like to see your idea come back to life after you thought it was dead?

According to the *Merriam-Webster Dictionary*, the word *ascension* means, "the act of moving to a higher or more powerful position."[7] How have some of your ideas ascended into reality? What did it stir in you to go through those experiences?

What does the pattern of Jesus teach you about obedience?

How are you practicing obedience in your current circumstances or situation?

Read Luke 24:1–53. In these verses, we read about the resurrection and ascension of Jesus. Notice the great joy and praise that comes *after* the ascension. Today, think about where you are at in the cycle of an idea, a daring dream, or a big ask. Ask God to give you the patience to be obedient to the life that he has for you. Thank God that he is with you every step of the way, and praise him for the great joy that comes when your idea, dreams, and asks become reality.

STAY TRUE

Perhaps the most challenging part of life isn't discovering what we're *for*—it's staying true to who we want to be and what we want to be known *for*. Challenging moments will eventually land before each of us. The question we need to ask is whether *we will stay true to what we're for or if we will make subtle compromises along the way.*

Chick-fil-A is still closed on Sundays. A large outdoor adventure retailer is closed every year on Black Friday. Your pastor takes a Sabbath day at some point every week—even in the midst of glaring needs in your church community. You unplug from your phone and email notifications for a few hours every night to get some sleep (or at least I hope you do!). The point is that there are *many choices* you make every day to stay true to who you are, to the mission of your ministry, or to the vision of your organization—even when you have to make sacrifices at the expense of some*one* or some*thing* else.

Staying true in those moments is what allows you to bring your best and encourage the best in others. It's actually a great way to be *for* your world, *for* your team, *for* your community, and ultimately *for* your life. You live the life God has *for* you with your fullest potential by staying true. Consider what this looks like for you as you answer the following questions.

What does staying true and avoiding compromises look like for you?

What opportunities or challenges make staying true hard for you?

Think about someone in your life who models this concept well. What do you admire about that person's commitment to stay true?

Have you ever been frustrated or inconvenienced by someone else's decision to stay true? (Like pulling into Chick-fil-A on a Sunday?)

What happens when you don't stay true? Is there an example from your own experience or the experience of someone around you?

How does the life of Jesus inspire you to stay true?

What opportunities or challenges may have made it hard for Jesus to stay true?

How do you encourage others to stay true to the life God has for them?

Read Hebrews 12:1–3. The author of this letter wrote these words to encourage all believers in Christ to stay committed and true to the life God had called them to live. Consider how these words encourage you today. Thank God for the gift of perseverance as you run your own race, and ask him to show you the joy he has set before you so you don't grow weary and lose heart. And thank him for the courage he gives you to stay true to the life he has *for* you.

FOR YOU

For some of us, it's hard to imagine a loving God who wants us to live our best life. We move throughout our days thinking the life God has for us is the exact *opposite* of our best life. Perhaps this is the message we grew up with in our family of origin or the impression we received from an unhealthy faith community experience.

The effects of this way of thinking lead us to believe that God's version of our best life is one of suffering, hardship, and misery. We keep God at arm's length—because if we get too close, we fear we will have to live that bad life and fool ourselves into thinking it's good. But the Bible tells us that we serve a God who delights in us and longs to give us the desires of our heart (see Psalm 37:4). So, with this in mind, here are a few questions to consider as you move forward and live the life God has for you—your best life.

Are you at a sustainable pace in life? If not, what pace would take you to a better place?

Are you giving yourself enough time and space to *think*? If not, what changes could you make to your schedule to allow more time for just thinking?

How are you prepping for your day? How would things change at the start of your day if you took time to prep the night before?

Who in your life is sharpening, challenging, and inspiring you? Do you already have a mentor? Is there someone who comes to mind as a potential mentor?

What are you "asking big" for in your life?

Have you found your voice in your community? If so, how are you exercising that voice?

How are you practicing humility?

Do you feel you are living the best life God has for you? If not, what are you waiting for?

Finish Strong: Use the space below to write down any key insights or questions from your personal study that you want to discuss if your group decides to continue meeting. Otherwise, visit JeffHenderson.com for additional resources regarding how you can help your business or nonprofit organization grow with the strategic principles found in the *Know What You're For* book.

EPILOGUE

Some of the best communication advice I have been given is to state at the beginning what I want to say at the end. So, here's the deal: *The future is a blank page where you get to write your answer. So write it well.*

Maybe you are a little confused on how to write a good life. Or maybe you've had a few setbacks and false starts and you are hesitant to begin again. Like the time you failed at a new business venture or asked for something big but never got it. Or maybe you wanted to have a baby, or get that job promotion, or be healed from an illness, or make the varsity team, but life didn't work out that way for you. Or perhaps you thought you had life all figured out and were living it well . . . but something in this study has stirred things up for you.

So now what? How do you start fresh or stay true and live a good life? Here's my answer: *When you get crystal clear on what you want to be known for, every square inch of your life becomes an opportunity to live out that answer . . . and this is how you write it well.*

So let's get crystal clear on what it looks like for you to write your life well by determining your answers to the two key questions of this study: (1) *What are you for?* and (2) *What are you known for*—in your world, your relationships, and your community? God wants you to live the life he has for you, and when you do this, it has ripple effects in every other area of your life.

Do you want to be known as a loving person? Jesus says, "Remain in me." Do you want to be known as a trustworthy leader? Jesus says, "Remain in me." Do you want to be known as a team player? Jesus says, "Remain in me." Do you want to be known as a wise parent or mentor? Jesus says, "Remain in me." This is how you stay true to the life God has *for* you.

Your obedience to Jesus is what allows you to close the gap between what you're *for* and what you're *known for*. This is true for all of us in our personal and professional lives. And it's true of our business environments, our community organizations, and our local churches. *We write a good life when we live in obedience to Jesus.*

So, in an often hypercritical and cynical world, let's practice what we have learned here together—be known more for who and what we're *for* rather than who and what we're against. It's a simple but powerful way to live.

Thank you for your willingness to lead your group through this study! What you have chosen to do is valuable and will make a great difference in the lives of others. The rewards of being a leader are different from those of participating, and we hope that as you lead you will find your own walk with Jesus deepened by this experience.

Know What You're FOR is a five-session study built around video content and small-group interaction. As the group leader, just think of yourself as the host of a dinner party. Your job is to take care of your guests by managing all the behind-the-scenes details so that when everyone arrives, they can just enjoy time together.

As the group leader, your role is not to answer all the questions or reteach the content—the video, book, and study guide will do most of that work. Your job is to guide the experience and cultivate your small group into a kind of teaching community. This will make it a place for members to process, question, and reflect—not receive more instruction.

Before your first meeting, make sure everyone in the group gets a copy of the study guide. This will keep everyone on the same page and help the process run more smoothly. If some group members are unable to purchase the guide, arrange it so that people can share the resource with other group members. Giving everyone access to all the material will position this study to be as rewarding an experience as possible. Everyone should feel free to write in his or her study guide and bring it to group every week.

SETTING UP THE GROUP

You will need to determine with your group how long you want to meet each week so you can plan your time accordingly. Generally, most groups like to meet for either ninety minutes or two hours, so you could use one of the following schedules:

SECTION	90 MIN.	120 MIN.
Welcome (members arrive and get settled)	10 min.	15 min.
Share (discuss one or more of the opening questions for the session)	10 min.	15 min.
Read (discuss the questions based on the Scripture reading for the week)	10 min.	15 min.
Watch (watch the teaching material together and take notes)	20 min.	20 min.
Discuss (discuss the Bible study questions you selected ahead of time)	30 min.	40 min.
Respond / Pray (pray together as a group and dismiss)	10 min.	15 min.

As the group leader, you'll want to create an environment that encourages sharing and learning. A church sanctuary or formal classroom may not be as ideal as a living room, because those locations can feel formal and less intimate. No matter what setting you choose, provide enough comfortable seating for everyone, and, if possible, arrange the seats in a semicircle so everyone can see the video easily. This will make the transition between the video and group conversation more efficient and natural.

Also, try to get to the meeting site early so you can greet participants as they arrive. Simple refreshments create a welcoming atmosphere and can be a wonderful addition to a group study evening. Try to take food and pet allergies into account to make your guests as comfortable as possible. You may also want to consider offering childcare to couples with children who want to attend. Finally, be sure your media technology is working properly. Managing these details up front will make the rest of your group experience flow smoothly and provide a welcoming space in which to engage the content of *Know What You're FOR*.

STARTING THE GROUP TIME

Once everyone has arrived, it's time to begin the group. Here are some simple tips to make your group time healthy, enjoyable, and effective.

First, begin the meeting with a short prayer and remind the group members to put their phones on silent. This is a way to make sure you can all be present with one another and with God. Next, give each person a few minutes to respond to the questions in the "Share" and "Read" sections. This won't require as much time in session one, but beginning in session two, people will need more time to share their insights from their personal studies. Usually, you won't answer the discussion questions yourself, but you should go first with the "Share" and "Read" questions, answering briefly and with a reasonable amount of transparency.

At the end of session one, invite the group members to complete the between-sessions personal studies for that week. Explain that you will be providing some time before the video teaching next week for anyone to share insights. Let them know sharing is optional, and it's no problem if they can't get to some of the between-sessions activities some weeks. It will still be beneficial for them to hear from the other participants and learn about what they discovered.

LEADING THE DISCUSSION TIME

Now that the group is engaged, it's time to watch the video and respond with some directed small-group discussion. Encourage all the group members to participate in the discussion, but make sure they know they don't have to do so. As the discussion progresses, you may want to follow up with comments such as, "Tell me more about that," or, "Why did you answer that way?" This will allow the group participants to deepen their reflections and invite meaningful sharing in a nonthreatening way.

Note that you have been given multiple questions to use in each session, and you do not have to use them all or even follow them in order. Feel free to pick and choose questions based on either the needs of your group or how the conversation is flowing. Also, don't be afraid of silence. Offering a question and allowing up to thirty seconds of silence is okay. It allows people space to think about how they want to respond and also gives them time to do so.

As group leader, you are the boundary keeper for your group. Do not let anyone (yourself included) dominate the group time. Keep an eye out for group members who might be tempted to "attack" folks they disagree with or try to "fix" those having struggles. These kinds of behaviors can derail a group's momentum, so they need to be steered in a different direction. Model active listening and encourage everyone in your group to do the same. This will make your group time a safe space and create a positive community.

The group discussion leads to a closing time of individual reflection and prayer. Encourage the participants to take a few moments to review what they've learned during the session and write down their thoughts to the "Respond" section. This will help them cement the big ideas in their minds as you close the session. Conclude by having the participants break into smaller groups of two to three people to pray for one another.

Thank you again for taking the time to lead your group. You are making a difference in the lives of others and having an impact on the kingdom of God!

ENDNOTES

1. Annie Dillard, *The Writing Life* (New York: HarperCollins, 1989).
2. John Maxwell, foreword to *Know What You're FOR* (Grand Rapids, MI: Zondervan, 2019).
3. *Merriam-Webster Dictionary*, "Definition of Strategy," https://www.merriam-webster.com/dictionary/strategy.
4. Jeff Henderson and Sid Mashburn, "016: Sid Mashburn on Launching the Number One Men's Independent Clothing Store in the US Pt. 1," February 2, 2017, *Launch Youniversity*, podcast, https://launchyouniversity.com/podcast/016-sid-mashburn-launching-number-one-mens-independent-clothing-store-us-pt-1.
5. Cheryl Bachelder, "Five Traits of Leaders Who Serve," *Serving Performs*, November 1, 2012, https://cherylbachelder.com/servant-leadership/five-traits-of-leaders-who-serve/.
6. For more on David, visit www.launchyouniversity.com.
7. *Merriam-Webster Dictionary*, "Definition of Ascension," https://www.merriam-webster.com/dictionary/ascension.

Know What You're FOR

A Growth Strategy for Work, An Even Better Strategy for Life

Jeff Henderson

"Jeff is the real deal. I have long admired the way he leads, and this book does not disappoint."

—MARK BATTERSON, New York Times bestselling author of *The Circle Maker*

"Jeff's ideas will be transformational for you and your team."

—TIM TASSOPOULOS, president and COO, Chick-fil-A, Inc.

"This is the book you've been waiting for to take your team to places you've never been while living a beautiful life in the process."

—LYSA TERKEURST, #1 *New York Times* bestselling author and president of Proverbs 31 Ministries

Unprecedented growth is no longer about being the best company IN the world but about being the best company FOR the world.

We know word-of-mouth advertising is the secret to thriving businesses and communities, but too often it seems so elusive, even mysterious. Business leader and entrepreneur Jeff Henderson, says it's time to rethink how to grow your business.

From three decades of working with organizations like Chick-fil-A, the Atlanta Braves, and North Point Ministries, Jeff reveals a simple and profoundly powerful strategy for generating free, positive, word-of-mouth advertising. Not only is this a growth strategy for work; it's an even better strategy for life.

Available in stores and online!